CREATION

CREATION

And God said,
"Let There Be Light!"

By
Annie N. Mundeke, Ph.D.

iUniverse, Inc.
New York Bloomington

Creation
And God said, "Let There Be Light!"

iUniverse books may be ordered through booksellers or by contacting:

iUniverse
1663 Liberty Drive
Bloomington, IN 47403
www.iuniverse.com
1-800-Authors (1-800-288-4677)

ISBN: 978-1-4502-1108-6 (sc)
ISBN: 978-1-4502-1109-3 (ebk)

Printed in the United States of America

iUniverse rev. date: 11/16/2011

And God said, "Let There Be Light!"

—*Genesis 1:3*

[14] And God said, "Let there be lights in the expanse of the sky to separate the day from the night, and let them serve as signs to mark seasons and days and years, [15] and let them be lights in the expanse of the sky to give light on the earth." And it was so. [16] God made two great lights—the greater light to govern the day and the lesser light to govern the night. He also made the stars. [17] God set them in the expanse of the sky to give light on the earth, [18] to govern the day and the night, and to separate light from darkness. And God saw that it was good. [19] And there was evening, and there was morning—the fourth day

—*Genesis 1:14*

The Word Became Flesh

¹In the beginning was the Word, and the Word was with God, and the Word was God. ²He was with God in the beginning.
³Through him all things were made; without him nothing was made that has been made. ⁴In him was life, and that life was the light of men. ⁵The light shines in the darkness, but the darkness has not understood[a] it.

—John 1-1-5

Age group: Boys and girls from 8 to 13 years old.

To God, our Creator, our Lord and Savior, Jesus Christ.

Contents

Preface

God exists.

God created us.

God is good.

God is our Creator.

God has only one Begotten Son, the Lord Jesus Christ.

The Lord Jesus Christ is the only Begotten Son of God.

The Lord Jesus Christ is the only Begotten Son of God.

The Lord Jesus Christ is God.

The Lord Jesus Christ created us.

The Lord Jesus Christ created all the peoples in the world.

The Lord Jesus Christ created everything in the world.

The Lord Jesus Christ is God, our Creator.

The Lord Jesus Christ is God of Creation.

The Lord Jesus Christ created the world.

The Lord Jesus Christ created everything in the world.

The Lord Jesus Christ is God.

God is our Creator.

God created the world and everything in it.

God created men and women.

God created all the peoples in the world.

God Created you and me!

God created the light!

> And God said, "Let there be light," and there was light.
>
> —Genesis 1:3

Acknowledgments

My special thanks go to God, our Creator, your Creator, our Lord and Savior, Jesus Christ.

My special thanks also go to my mother and my father Mom, Magdalene Kayowa Mundeke and to Dad, Albert Mundeke Yakalenge.

Last, not least my special thanks go to my brothers, sisters, friends, and church family.

Notes from the author

God exists. He is our Creator. God loves us.

God exists.

There is God.

God is good.

Good is awesome.

God is our Creator.

God created us.

God created us in His image: So God created mankind in his own image, in the image of God he created them; male and female he created them [Genesis 1:27].

God loves us.

God created all peoples.

God created everything [John 1-14].

Thank You, God, for Your creation.

Thank You, God, for creating everything.

Thank You, God, for creating all the peoples.

Thank You, God, for creating me!

Thank You, God, for creating light!

God is good; He created light!

And God said, "Let there be light," and there was light

—Genesis 1:3

Wow! *Wow!* *Wow!* *Wow!*

Wow! *Wow!* *Wow!* *Wow!*

Joy! *Joy!* *Joy!* *Joy!*

Joy! *Joy!* *Joy!* *Joy!*

Joy! *Joy!* *Joy!* *Joy!*

Please, color this picture in blue

Introduction

In the beginning was the Word, and the Word was with God, and the Word was God.

—John 1:1

God exists.

There is God.

God is our Creator.

God created the world and everything in it [Acts 17:24]. God created man.

God created the world in six days!

In six days, God created the world.

God exists! *Yes!*

There is God! *Yes!*

God spoke the world into existence

(John 1:1-5).

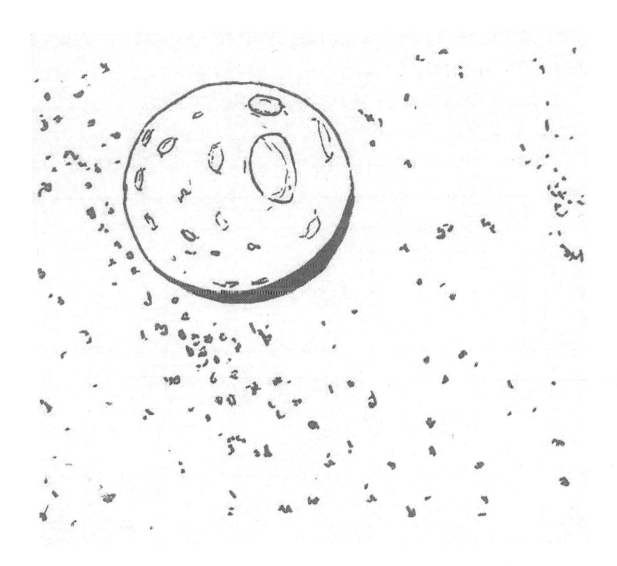

Please, color this picture

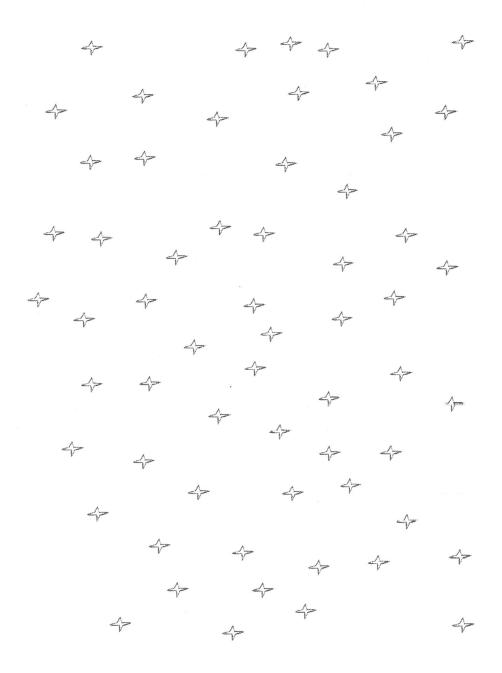

Lesson to Learn : God exists! There is God! God is Our Creator! God loves us!

Lesson 1
What God Created on the First Day

Light
Genesis 1:3

God exists.

God is our Creator.

There is God.

God created us.

God is our Creator.

God spoke the world into existence.

God created the world in six days!

In six days, God created the world.

Wow! Wow! Wow!

God spoke the world into existence.

Annie N. Mundeke, Ph.D.

God created the universe.

God created men in His image.

God created you and me.

Wow!   *Wow!*   *Wow!*

Wow!   *Wow!*   *Wow!*

God spoke the world into existence.

The Word Became Flesh

[1]In the beginning was the Word, and the Word was with God, and the Word was God.
[2]He was with God in the beginning.
[3]Through him all things were made; without him nothing was made that has been made.
[4]In him was life, and that life was the light of men.
[5]The light shines in the darkness, but the darkness has not understood[a] it

—*John 1:1-5*

God created the world. God created the light

Lesson to Learn 1: God exists. There is God.

Wow! Wow! Wow! Wow!

Please, color this picture in blue

Lesson 2
What God Created on the Second Day

The Heavens and the Earth

The Heavens

God created the heavens and the earth

[1] In the beginning God created the heavens and the earth.

[2] Now the earth was [a] formless and empty, darkness was over the surface of the deep, and the Spirit of God was hovering over the waters.

[3] And God said, "Let there be light," and there was light.

[4] God saw that the light was good, and He separated the light from the darkness.

[5] God called the light "day," and the darkness he called "night." And there was evening, and there was morning—the first day.

—Genesis 1:1-5

God created water.

[6] And God said, "Let there be an expanse between the waters to separate water from water."

[7] So God made the expanse and separated the water under

the expanse from the water above it. And it was so.
⁸ God called the expanse "sky." And there was evening, and there was morning—the second day.
⁹ And God said, "Let the water under the sky be gathered to one place, and let dry ground appear." And it was so.
¹⁰ God called the dry ground "land," and the gathered waters he called "seas." And God saw that it was good.

—Genesis 1:6-10

God created water.

Yes! Yes!

Joy! Joy!

Lesson to Learn 2: God created the heavens and the earth.

Yes! Yes!

Lesson 3
What God Created on the Third Day

Vegetation (Trees and Gardens)

God created vegetation.

> [11] Then God said, "Let the land produce vegetation: seed-bearing plants and trees on the land that bear fruit with seed in it, according to their various kinds." And it was so.
>
> [12] The land produced vegetation: plants bearing seed according to their kinds and trees bearing fruit with seed in it according to their kinds. And God saw that it was good.
>
> [13] And there was evening, and there was morning—the third day.
>
> —*Genesis 1:11-13*

God created vegetation (trees and gardens)

Plants, flowers! Beauty!

Beauty! Beauty! Beauty!

Lesson to Learn 3: God created all plants and all flowers. God created the vegetation.

Lesson 4
What God Created on the Fourth Day

The Lights of the Heavens

God created the light.

> ¹⁴ And God said, "Let there be lights in the expanse of the sky to separate the day from the night, and let them serve as signs to mark seasons and days and years,
> ¹⁵ and let them be lights in the expanse of the sky to give light on the earth." And it was so.
> ¹⁶ God made two great lights—the greater light to govern the day and the lesser light to govern the night. He also made the stars.
> ¹⁷ God set them in the expanse of the sky to give light on the earth,
> ¹⁸ to govern the day and the night, and to separate light from darkness. And God saw that it was good.
> ¹⁹ And there was evening, and there was morning—the fourth day.
>
> —*Genesis 1:14-19*

The light was created by God.

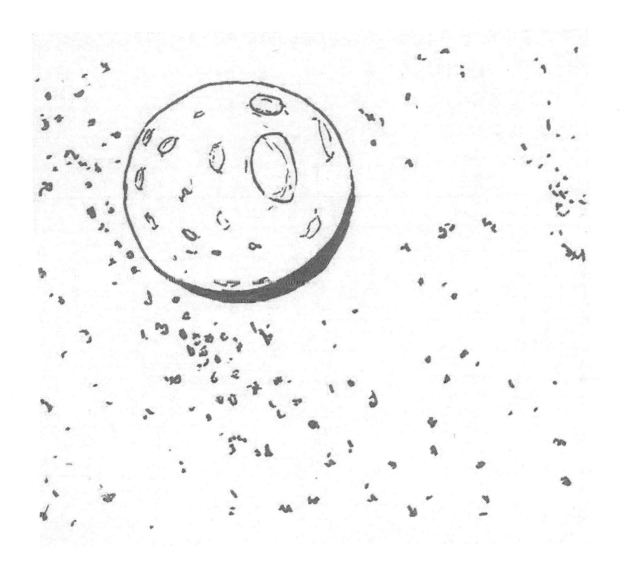

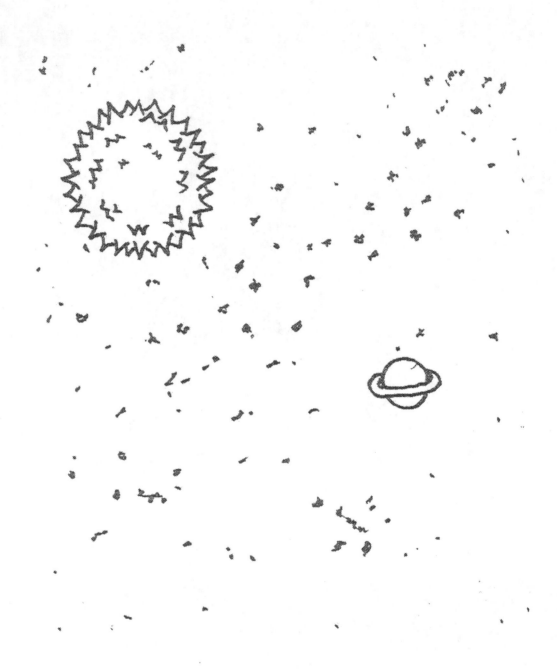

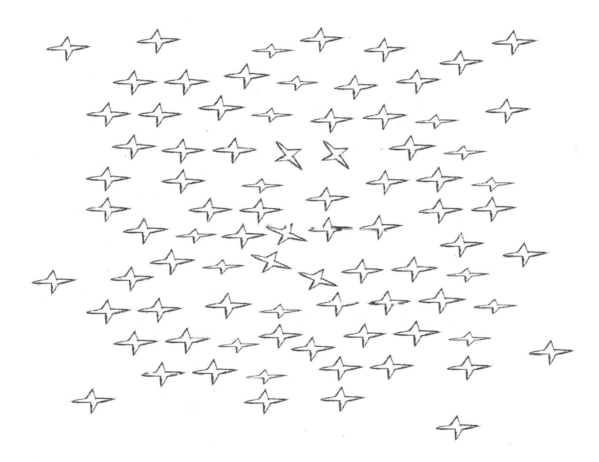

Annie N. Mundeke, Ph.D.

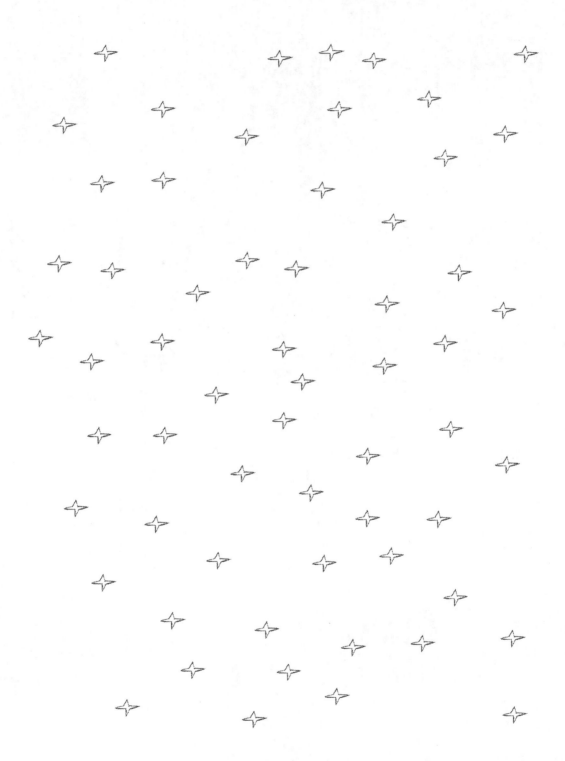

Lesson to learn from chapter 4:

Joy! Joy! Joy! Joy!

Joy! Joy! Joy! Joy!

Joy! Joy! Joy! Joy!

Lesson 5
What God Created on the Fifth Day

Sea Creatures

Birds

Animals

God created animals.

20 And God said, "Let the water teem with living creatures, and let birds fly above the earth across the expanse of the sky."
21 So God created the great creatures of the sea and every living and moving thing with which the water teems, according to their kinds, and every winged bird according to its kind. And God saw that it was good.
22 God blessed them and said, "Be fruitful and increase in number and fill the water in the seas, and let the birds increase on the earth."
23 And there was evening, and there was morning—the fifth day.

24 And God said, "Let the land produce living creatures according to their kinds: livestock, creatures that move along the ground, and wild animals, each according to

its kind." And it was so.

25 God made the wild animals according to their kinds, the livestock according to their kinds, and all the creatures that move along the ground according to their kinds. And God saw that it was good.

—Genesis 1:20-24

Lesson to Learn 5: God created animals.

Nice! Nice! Nice! Nice! Yep!!

Lesson 6
What God Created on the Sixth Day

Man
Adam and Eve

God created man.

26 Then God said, "Let us make man in our image, in our likeness, and let them rule over the fish of the sea and the birds of the air, over the livestock, over all the earth, [b] and over all the creatures that move along the ground."

27 So God created man in his own image, in the image of God he created him; male and female he created them.

—*Genesis 1: 26-27*

God blessed man.

28 God blessed them and said to them, "Be fruitful and increase in number; fill the earth and subdue it. Rule over the fish of the sea and the birds of the air and over every living creature that moves on the ground."

29 Then God said, "I give you every seed-bearing plant on the face of the whole earth and every tree that has

fruit with seed in it. They will be yours for food.

[30] And to all the beasts of the earth and all the birds of the air and all the creatures that move on the ground—everything that has the breath of life in it—I give every green plant for food." And it was so.

[31] God saw all that he had made, and it was very good. And there was evening, and there was morning—the sixth day.

—Genesis 1:28- 31 31

Lesson to Learn 6: God created the lights of the heavens. God created all the lights! The Sun, the Moon, the stars and all of the lights of the heavens. You name it!

Adam and Eve

Lesson 7
What God Did on the Seventh Day

God rested on the seventh day.

No work!

God rested!

Genesis 2
¹ Thus the heavens and the earth were completed in all their vast array.
² By the seventh day God had finished the work he had been doing; so on the seventh day he rested [a] from all his work. ³ And God blessed the seventh day and made it holy, because on it he rested from all the work of creating that he had done.

—*Genesis 2:1-3*

Lesson to Learn 7: God rested on the 7ᵗʰ Day, therefore we need to rest. Rest is very important for our health.

Conclusion
God created the world. God created the world and everything in it [Acts 17:24]

God exists. [John 1:1-5]

God is our Creator. [John 1:1-5], [Genesis 1:1]

There is God. [Genesis 1:1]

God created the heavens and the earth. [Genesis 1:1]

God created the world and everything in it. [Acts 17:24]

God created animals. [Genesis 1:24]

God created the heavens and the earth. [Genesis 1:1]

God created the water. [Genesis 1:20]

God created the light. [Genesis 1:3: 1:14]

God said: "Let there be light"! [Genesis 1: 3; 1:14]

God created the world by the power of His Word. [John 1:1-5; Colossians 1:1-15; Genesis 1:1-31].

God created the heavens and the earth. [Genesis 1:1]

God created the light:

> 13 And God said, "Let there be light," and there was light [Genesis 1:3].
>
> 14 And God said, "Let there be lights in the expanse of the sky to separate the day from the night, and let them serve as signs to mark seasons and days and years,
>
> 15 and let them be lights in the expanse of the sky to give light on the earth." And it was so.
>
> 16 God made two great lights—the greater light to govern the day and the lesser light to govern the night. He also made the stars.
>
> 17 God set them in the expanse of the sky to give light on the earth, 18 to govern the day and the night, and to separate light from darkness. And God saw that it was good.
>
> 19 And there was evening, and there was morning—the fourth day.
>
> *—Genesis 1:14-19*

God created Adam and Eve, our first parents [Genesis 1:27; Genesis 2:21].

Concluding Remarks

God exists. God created us. God is our Creator.
God spoke the world into existence.
Read the Holy Bible.

Genesis 1

The Beginning

¹ In the beginning God created the heavens and the earth.

² Now the earth was [a] formless and empty, darkness was over the surface of the deep, and the Spirit of God was hovering over the waters.

³ And God said, "Let there be light," and there was light.

⁴ God saw that the light was good, and He separated the light from the darkness.

⁵ God called the light "day," and the darkness he called "night." And there was evening, and there was morning—the first day.

⁶ And God said, "Let there be an expanse between the waters to separate water from water."

⁷ So God made the expanse and separated the water under the expanse from the water above it. And it was so.

⁸ God called the expanse "sky." And there was evening, and there was morning—the second day.

⁹ And God said, "Let the water under the sky be gathered to one place, and let dry ground appear." And it was so.

¹⁰ God called the dry ground "land," and the gathered waters he called "seas." And God saw that it was good.

¹¹ Then God said, "Let the land produce vegetation: seed-bearing plants and trees on the land that bear fruit with seed in it, according to their various kinds." And it was so.

¹² The land produced vegetation: plants bearing seed according to their kinds and trees bearing fruit with seed in it according to their kinds. And God saw that it was good.

¹³ And there was evening, and there was morning—the third day.

¹⁴ And God said, "Let there be lights in the expanse of the sky to separate the day from the night, and let them serve as signs to mark seasons and days and years,

¹⁵ and let them be lights in the expanse of the sky to give light on the earth." And it was so.

¹⁶ God made two great lights—the greater light to govern the day and the lesser light to govern the night. He also made the stars.

¹⁷ God set them in the expanse of the sky to give light on the earth,

¹⁸ to govern the day and the night, and to separate light from darkness. And God saw that it was good.

¹⁹ And there was evening, and there was morning—the fourth day.

²⁰ And God said, "Let the water teem with living creatures, and let birds fly above the earth across the expanse of the sky."

²¹ So God created the great creatures of the sea and every living and moving thing with which the water teems, according to their kinds, and every winged bird according to its kind. And God saw that it was good.

²² God blessed them and said, "Be fruitful and increase in number and fill the water in the seas, and let the birds increase on the earth."

²³ And there was evening, and there was morning—the fifth day.

²⁴ And God said, "Let the land produce living creatures according to their kinds: livestock, creatures that move along the ground, and wild animals, each according to its kind." And it was so.

²⁵ God made the wild animals according to their kinds, the livestock according to their kinds, and all the creatures that move along the ground according to their kinds. And God saw that it was good.

²⁶ Then God said, "Let us make man in our image, in our likeness, and let them rule over the fish of the sea and the birds of the air, over the livestock, over all the earth, [b] and over all the creatures that move along the ground."

²⁷ So God created man in his own image, in the image of God he created him male and female he created them.

²⁸ God blessed them and said to them, "Be fruitful and increase in number; fill the earth and subdue it. Rule over the fish of the sea and the birds of the air and over every living creature that moves on the ground."

²⁹ Then God said, "I give you every seed-bearing plant on the face of the whole earth and every tree that has fruit with seed in it. They will be yours for food.

³⁰ And to all the beasts of the earth and all the birds of the air and all the creatures that move on the ground—everything that has the breath of life in it—I give every green plant for food." And it was so.

³¹ God saw all that he had made, and it was very good. And there was evening, and there was morning—the sixth day [Genesis 1: 1-31].

The Blue Sky. Please color in Blue

Activities to do after the reading

Day 1

- Who is our Creator?

....

....

....

- What did God create on the first day?

....

....

....

....

....

....

....

....

....

....

....

- How do we know God exists and that He is our Creator?

....

....

....

....

....

....

....

....

- What verse or verses of the Scriptures teach us that God exists and that He is our Creator?

....

....

....

....

....

....

Day 2

- What did God create on the second day?

....

....

....

....

....

....

....

....

....

....

....

....

....

....

....

Day 3

- What did God create on the third day?

....

....

....

....

....

....

....

....

....

....

....

....

....

....

....

Day 4

- What did God create on the fourth day?

....

....

....

....

....

....

....

....

....

....

....

....

....

....

Day 5

- What did God create on the fifth day?

....

....

....

....

....

....

....

....

....

....

....

....

....

....

....

Day 6

- What did God create on the sixth day?

....

....

....

....

....

....

....

....

....

....

....

....

....

....

....

Day 7

- What did God do on the seventh day?

....

....

....

....

....

....

....

....

....

....

....

....

....

....

....

....

The Book of Genesis

Answers to the questions (notes from the Internet).

Please read to enrich your knowledge.

Genesis 1

Genesis 1:1. Who created the heavens and the earth?
God.

Genesis 1:1. What did God create in the very beginning?
The heavens and the earth.

Genesis 1:2. Describe the earth in the very beginning. What was over the deep? What was hovering over the waters?
Formless and empty•—darkness was over the deep—the Spirit of God was over the waters.

Genesis 1:3-5. What did God create on the first day and what did He do with this creation?
Light; He separated the light from the darkness.

Genesis 1:5. What did God call the light and darkness He created on the first day?
Day and night.

Genesis 1:5. What did the first day consist of after God created day and night?
Evening and morning.

Genesis 1:6-8. What did God create on the second day and what did He do with this creation?
The sky; separated the water from the sky.

Genesis 1:6-8. What did God use to separate water from water and what did He name it?
An expanse; the sky.

Genesis 1:9-13. What did God create on the third day?
Separated water on earth and made land; made vegetation on the land.

Genesis 1:9-10. What did God call the dry ground He made appear between the waters?
Land.

Genesis 1:9-10. What did God call the water He had gathered together to make land?
The seas.

Genesis 1:11-12. When God made vegetation on the land, what did this include?
Plants bearing seed according to their kind and trees bearing fruit with seeds in it according to their kinds.

Genesis 1:14-19. What did God create on the fourth day?
Lights in the sky to separate day from night, greater light in the day, lesser light at night, and the stars.

Genesis 1:14. Besides letting the lights in the sky serve to separate night from day, what other purpose would they serve?
As signs to mark the seasons, days, and years.

Genesis 1:20-23. What did God create on the fifth day?
Living creatures of the water, winged creatures of the air.

Genesis 1:22. What blessing did God place upon the creatures of the water and air?

Be fruitful, increase in number, and fill the water in the seas; let the birds increase on the earth.

Genesis 1:24-31. What did God create on the sixth day?

Living creatures on land—animals, man in his image.

Genesis 1:24. When God created living creatures on land, what kind of living creatures did this mean?

Livestock, creatures that move along the ground, wild animals.

Genesis 1:26. In whose image was man made?

God's.

Genesis 1:26. Over what did God make man the ruler?

The fish of the sea, the birds of the air, livestock, all the earth, and all the creatures that move along the ground.

Genesis 1:28. What blessing did God place upon man just after creating him?

Be fruitful and increase in number, fill the earth and subdue it, rule over the fish of the sea and over the birds of the air and over all of the creatures that move along the ground.

Genesis 1:29. What did God give man for food?

Every seed-bearing plant on the face of the earth and every tree that has fruit with seed in it.

Genesis 1:30. What did God give "everything that has the breath of life in it" for food?

Every green plant.

Genesis 1:30. What animals did God include in the statement "everything that has the breath of life in it"?
All the beasts of the earth, all the birds of the air, all the creatures that move along the ground.

Genesis 2:2. What did God do on the seventh day, and why?
He rested because He had finished all of His work.

Genesis 2:3. What did God do to the seventh day because that was when <u>He rested?</u>
He blessed it and made it holy.

Genesis 2

Genesis 2:4-7. What was the earth like when God created man?
No shrub of the field had yet appeared on the earth, no plant of the field had yet sprung up, God had not yet sent rain, no man to work the ground, streams came up from the earth and watered the whole surface.

Genesis 2:7. What did God form man out of?
The dust of the ground.

Genesis 2:7. Where did God breathe into man the breath of life?
His nostrils.

Genesis 2:8 - Where had God planted a garden? (General area and specific name)
In the East, in Eden.

Genesis 2:8. Where did God place the man that He had formed?
Garden of Eden.

Genesis 2:9. What kind of trees grew in the Garden of Eden?
Trees that were pleasing to the eye and good for food.

Genesis 2:9. What two trees were in the middle of the Garden of Eden?
The tree of life and the tree of the knowledge of good and evil.

Genesis 2:10. A river watering the garden flowed from Eden. How many headwaters was this river separated into?
Four.

Genesis 2:11. What land does the river <u>Pishon flow through?</u>
<u>Havilah.</u>

Answers to the Questions
For Activities

Day 1

- Who is our Creator?

  God.
  God is our Creator.
  God created us.

- What did God create on the first day?

  Light.

- How do we know God exists and that He is our Creator?

  His Word teaches us that <u>God…exists</u>
  Jesus teaches us that <u>God…exists</u>
  Nature teaches us that God…exists.

- What verse or verses of the Scriptures teach us that God exists and that He is our Creator?

  John 1:1-5.
  Genesis 1:27.

Day 2

- What did God create on the second day?

  The heavens.

Day 3

- What did God create on the third day?

  Trees and garden.
  Plants.
  (Vegetation.)

Day 4

- What did God create on the fourth day?

  Lights of heavens.
  The moon.
  The sun.
  The stars.

Day 5

- What did God create on the fifth day?

  Sea creatures.
  The birds and the animals.

Day 6

- What did God create on the sixth day?

  Man.
  Adam and Eve.

Day 7

- What did God do on the seventh day?

  God rested.

Elaborated Answers

Elaborated answers to the questions that are raised in this book are in the Holy Bible, in the book of Genesis, chapter 1, and Genesis, chapter 2. We also read powerful verses about who the Creator is, and His creation, in the book John 1:1-14.

Answers can also be found in the following pages, with notes from the Internet.

Notes from the Internet.

Genesis 1:1. Who created the heavens and the earth?
God.

Genesis 1:1. What did God create in the very beginning?
The heavens and the earth.

Genesis 1:2. Describe the earth in the very beginning. What was over the deep? What was hovering over the waters?
Formless and empty—darkness was over the deep—the Spirit of God was over the waters.

Genesis 1:3-5. What did God create on the first day and what did He do with this creation?
Light; He separated the light from the darkness.

Genesis 1:5. What did God call the light and darkness He created on the first day?
Day and night.

Genesis 1:5. What did the first day consist of after God created day and night?
Evening and morning.

Genesis 1:6-8. What did God create on the second day and what did He do with this creation?
The sky; separated the water from the sky.

Genesis 1:6-8. What did God use to separate water from water and what did He name it?
An expanse; the sky.

Genesis 1:9-13. What did God create on the third day?
Separated water on earth and made land, and made vegetation on the land.

Genesis 1:9-10. What did God call the dry ground He made appear between the waters?
Land.

Genesis 1:9-10. What did God call the water He had gathered together to make land?
The seas.

Genesis 1:11-12. When God made vegetation on the land what did this include?
Plants bearing seed according to their kind and trees bearing fruit with seeds in it according to their kind.

Genesis 1:14-19. What did God create on the fourth day?
Lights in the sky to separate day from night, greater light in the day, lesser one at night, and the stars.

Genesis 1:14. Besides letting the lights in the sky serve to separate night from day, what other purpose would they serve?
As signs to mark the seasons, days, and years.

Genesis 1:20-23. What did God create on the fifth day?
Living creatures of the water, winged creatures of the air.

Genesis 1:22. What blessing did God place upon the creatures of the water and air?
Be fruitful, increase in number, and fill the water in the seas; let the birds increase on the earth.

Genesis 1:24-31. What did God create on the sixth day?
Living creatures on land—animals, man in his image.

Genesis 1:24. When God created living creatures on land, what kind of living creatures did this mean?

This means that God created the Livestock, the creatures that move along the ground, the wild animals. Let us read in the Scriptures, the Word of God:

And God said, "Let the land produce living creatures according to their kinds: livestock, creatures that move along the ground, and wild animals, each according to its kind." And it was so (Genesis 1:24).

In the following verse, we read more about what God did when He created the animals

25 God made the wild animals according to their kinds, the livestock according to their kinds, and all the creatures that move along the ground according to their kinds. And God saw that it was good (Genesis 1:25).

Creation

Genesis 1

The Creation Story

The story of how God made everything is, naturally, at the very beginning of the Bible:

> **In the beginning God created the heavens and the earth. The earth was empty, a formless mass cloaked in darkness. And the Spirit of God was hovering over its surface. Then God said, "Let there be light," and there was light. And God saw that it was good. Then he separated the light from the darkness. God called the light "day" and the darkness "night."**
>
> —(NLT, *Genesis 1:1-5*)

That was the **first day** of God's creation.
On the **second day**, God created the sky.
On the **third day**, God created the land, the oceans, and all the plants.
On the **fourth day**, God created the sun, moon, and stars.
On the **fifth day**, God created the birds, fishes, and other sea creatures.
On the **sixth day**, God created all the land animals and people.
On the **seventh day**, God rested.

By the seventh day God had finished the work he had been doing; so on the seventh day he rested from all his work. And God blessed the seventh day and made it holy, because on it he rested from all the work of creating that he had done. (NIV, Genesis 2:2-3)

References

The Holy Bible. New International Version. International Bible Society. USA (2005).

Annie Mundeke Ngana. *Jesus Loves Children,* Vol. 1. Authorhouse. Bloomington, IN. 2005.

Annie Mundeke Ngana. *Jesus Loves Children,* Vol. 2. Authorhouse, Bloomington, IN. 2005.

Articles on Creation in six days downloaded from the Internet. Christian Bible Reference Site

www.ChristianBibleReference.org or www.Twopaths.com